It's Raining Cats and Dogs

on

Amy!!

Best barkings
& mighty meows —
from Pé.

It's Raining Cats and Dogs

Edited by
Pie Corbett

Illustrated by **Bee Willey**

Blackie Children's Books

BLACKIE CHILDREN'S BOOKS
Published by the Penguin Group
Penguin Books Ltd, 27 Wrights Lane, London W8 5TZ, England
Penguin Books USA Inc., 375 Hudson Street, New York, New York 10014, USA
Penguin Books Australia Ltd, Ringwood, Victoria, Australia
Penguin Books Canada Ltd, 10 Alcorn Avenue, Toronto, Ontario, Canada M4V 3B2
Penguin Books (NZ) Ltd, 182–190 Wairau Road, Auckland 10, New Zealand

Penguin Books Ltd, Registered Offices: Harmondsworth, Middlesex, England

First published 1994
1 3 5 7 9 10 8 6 4 2

Introduction copyright © Pie Corbett, 1994
This selection copyright © Pie Corbett, 1994
Illustrations copyright © Bee Willey, 1994

The Acknowledgements on pp. 95–6 constitute an extension of this copyright page

All rights reserved. Without limiting the rights under copyright reserved above, no part of this publication may be reproduced, stored in or introduced into a retrieval system, or transmitted, in any form or by any means (electronic, mechanical, photocopying, recording or otherwise), without the prior written permission of both the copyright owner and the above publisher of this book

Filmset in Linotron Plantin by
Rowland Phototypesetting Ltd, Bury St Edmunds, Suffolk

Printed and bound in Great Britain by
Butler & Tanner Ltd, Frome and London

A CIP catalogue record for this book is available from the British Library

ISBN 0–216–94103–2

Contents

Introduction   9

The Cat's Muse	PHILIP GROSS	11
Cats	SIMON ARMITAGE	13
Feline	KATHERINE GALLAGHER	14
Litter	SUE COWLING	15
Kitten	JAMES KIRKUP	16
Next Door's Cat	BRIAN MOSES	18
The Owl and the Astronaut	GARETH OWEN	19
The Cat Sat on the Mat	JOHN RICE	20
Sun a-Shine, Rain a-Fall	VALERIE BLOOM	22
Cat Drinking	JAMIE CLARK	23
You *translated by*	MICHAEL ROSEN	24
Night Cat	HELEN DUNMORE	25
Cat	MATT SIMPSON	26
Cat and Mouse	MATT SIMPSON	27
Mouse	ALEXIS LYKIARD	28
Alley Cat	ESTHER VALCK GEORGES	29
The Cat on the Wall	JOHN MOLE	30
Coal Fire in December	WES MAGEE	31
The Car Park Cat	GINA DOUTHWAITE	32
A Warning to Cat Owners	SUE TOWNSEND	33
A Case of Murder	VERNON SCANNELL	34
Cat and the Weather	MAY SWENSON	36
from *A Child's Christmas in Wales*	DYLAN THOMAS	38
Fog	CARL SANDBURG	40
If you,	KARLA KUSKIN	41
December Cat	ADRIAN MITCHELL	42
Cat	DAVE CALDER	43
It's Raining Cats and Dogs	PETER DIXON	45
Travel Posters from Thomas Fox Travel Agents	TONY MITTON	46

Poem	Susan David	48
A Little Night Music	Kit Wright	49
Dog's Life	Matt Simpson	50
I Have This Crazy Problem	Mohammed Khan	51
Dogma	Marianne Chipperfield	52
What's the Rush!	Ian Souter	53
Charlotte's Dog	Kit Wright	55
The Mother's Song	Eskimo	56
Solitary Song	Eskimo	57
Haiku	Issa	58
Dog in the Street	Ishikawa Takuboku	59
Doggerel	Dave Calder	60
It Takes the (Dog) Biscuit	Trevor Harvey	62
Greedy Dog	James Hurley	63
First Dog on the Moon	David Orme	65
Dog in Space	Matthew Sweeney	66
How to Get in the Dog-House	Gina Douthwaite	67
The Barkday Party	James Berry	68
A Dog in the Margin	John Coldwell	70
The Dark Avenger	Trevor Millum	73
I Do Not Understand	Karla Kuskin	75
King of Dogs	Julie O'Callaghan	76
A Dog's Life	Gareth Owen	78
Experiment in Puppy Love	Gina Douthwaite	81
The Dog Lovers	Spike Milligan	82
Burying the Dog in the Garden	Brian Patten	83
Dead Dog	Vernon Scannell	85
April Gale	Ivor Gurney	86
A Dog in the Quarry	Miroslav Holub	87
To My Dog	Adrian Mitchell	90
Index of Authors		93
Acknowledgements		95

Introduction

I found my first kittens in a barn one winter. There were two of them, one tabby and a scrawny black and white one. My dad said that we shouldn't move them but the next day when I went back the tabby was dead. Perhaps the mother cat had been killed in the cold. We took the black and white one home and that was the beginning.

We lived on a farm and there were always cats around. At one point we had twenty-seven. They would sleep in saucepans, doze on top of the plate-rack or curl up in cupboards.

There was Bismouth, who ate cheese and once got shut in the fridge by mistake. There was Mother Bood who lived to twenty-three, which in cat years is 161 years old! There were cats that climbed curtains and that would leap on to your back for a game. And cats that caught rats and rabbits.

Our dogs grew up with cats so they never chased them. Quite often cats and dogs would curl up together for warmth. And like cats, the dogs had their own characters – dogs that chased flies and barked at shadows, dogs that ate Stilton cheese, dogs that could sing and played football.

These poems celebrate two of our oldest and best of friends – the cat and the dog. When reading these poems you may feel, as I do, how at times we too behave like cats or dogs.

PIE CORBETT

The Cat's Muse

*And the fat
cat musing on the mat
sang*

(flat):

I'm a tabby flabby house cat, just a fusty ball of fur,
A never-caught-a-mouse cat with a rusty sort of purr.
But sit down on the hearth mat and watch the fire with me.
I'll show you some of the dark and wild cats up my family tree.

> Oh I'm no common-or-garden cat.
> There's something you might miss:
> the sabre teeth that I unsheath
> when I stretch and yawn like this.

Sheba was a temple cat in Tutankhamun's days.
She had a hundred priestesses and several hundred slaves.
She curled up on an altar on a bed of purple silk,
Off saucers made of beaten gold she dined on camel's milk.

> Oh I'm no common-or-garden cat.
> My pedigree tends to show.
> My tail is like a cobra
> when it lashes to and fro.

Captain Moggan was a ship's cat and he sailed the
  Spanish Main.
He went all the way round Cape Horn and made it
  home again.
His claws were sharp as cutlasses. His life was sharp
  and short.
He died in Valparaiso, leaving kittens in every port.

> Oh I'm no common-or-garden cat.
> Haven't you noticed my
> one lop ear like a pirate's hat
> that flops across my eye?

Greymalkin was a black magic cat with fur as slick as
  pitch.
She held covens in a cavern with a wild and wicked
  witch.
And when she went out hunting on a moonlit winter's
  night
The village folk would bar their doors and dogs
  dropped dead with fright.

> Oh I'm no common-or-garden cat.
> Who knows what I might do?
> You'd better keep me happy
> or I'll put a spell . . .
>   . . . on . . .
>   . . . YOU!

PHILIP GROSS

Cats

Are safe, and stealing sleep in quiet curls
around the house, keeping secrets to themselves,
easily. Their lips are sealed, their tails are question
   marks
or ride up behind them like dodgem car hooks.

We love cats. They shred the settee and we sit there
and let them, we buy them toys or collars with bells
   on,
we give them our names and the warmest places
and behind our backs they are licking their faces.

The last cat to cross my path was a white one,
at night. Fast and silent like a shooting star
till it stopped, looked me up and down and blinked
then walked away, as if I was no one, leaving me cold

as if I'd been caught, or photographed, or shot at,
or had my wallet stolen. Cats are something else,
worlds away, and we are welcome to it,
this lump of rock in space we call our planet.

SIMON ARMITAGE

Feline

A coathanger body
arching tall

A multicoloured fuzz
on a garden-bench

A mewling voice
in a chorus-line

A pair of disco-eyes
to hex the dark

A tiger-chase
waiting for the call

A ball of fur
in a circle of sleep

KATHERINE GALLAGHER

Litter

Too old for kittens, not yet cats – cattens perhaps, or kits?

Matilda, the most cunning, hunts with eyes like watchtower slits.
O'Sullivan, the fighter, opens out his claws and spits
At Clarence chasing round and round as if he'd lost his wits,
While mischief-maker Millicent unpicks what Grandma knits
And spiteful Wilhelmina tears a butterfly to bits.

But Williams, who's the wisest and the cleverest, just – sits.

Sue Cowling

Kitten
(from 'Kitten on the Keys')

Broo, braa, bromm . . .
the tiny tom
cat
starts to pat
the chilly plush
of black and white –
the teeth of ivory
the bones of ebony.

What is this funny snow
that speaks?

Tilt head and listen
with round eyes
to keyboard dance,
to each
footfall dissonance –
a musical pounce
or a tricky bounce
or sweep your tail
along the scale.

Twitch ears

and whiskers
then slow
legato
sniff the keys –

someone you know
touched these.

JAMES KIRKUP

Next Door's Cat

Next door's cat lost
a couple of lives tonight.
Serve him right for
hanging around our pond,
seeking some fresh fish dish
to supplement his diet.

So out I crept behind the shed,
then slid on my belly, crocodile style,
while my target eyeballed the pond.

And I let him have just one more moment
of peace and contemplation,
before I let him have it . . .

I LEAPT and I ROARED,
I HOLLERED and I YELLED,
I WARDANCED and I SCREAMED,
I YAHOOED and I SCREEEEEEEEEECHED . . .

And I *swear* I saw a miracle
out there in our back garden,
when next door's cat *walked on water*
to escape the wrath of a demon.

Brian Moses

The Owl and the Astronaut

The owl and the astronaut
Sailed through space
In their intergalactic ship
They kept hunger at bay
With three pills a day
And drank through a protein drip.
The owl dreamed of mince
And slices of quince
And remarked how life had gone flat;
'It may be all right
To fly faster than light
But I preferred the boat and the cat.'

GARETH OWEN

The Cat Sat on the Mat . . . then he decided he'd go into the kitchen to see if there was any catfood in his dish but there wasn't any so he had an adventure with the food mixer which of course he shouldn't have touched because it's a very dangerous thing to play about with and he had been well warned but you know what cats are like, they get into everything. Anyway I know this is a long title so here comes the poem . . . oh by the way because I have made the title so long I have cut everything out of the poem except the rhyming words as I know you'll be tired reading all this.

.... mixer,
.... broken.
.... Trixer
.... soaken!

.... cat
.... jumps!
.... fat
.... lumps!

.... mixer,
.... faulty
.... Trixer
.... salty!

.... cat
.... wince
.... fat
.... mince!!!

JOHN RICE

Sun a-Shine, Rain a-Fall

Sun a-shine an' rain a-fall.
The Devil an' him wife cyan 'gree at all.
The two o' them want one fish-head.
The Devil: call him wife bonehead.
She hiss her teeth, call him cock-eye,
Greedy, worthless an' workshy.
While them busy callin' name,
The puss walk in, sey is a shame
To see a nice fish go to was'e,
Lef' with a big grin 'pon him face.

VALERIE BLOOM

Cat Drinking

He goes
lap after lap after lap
like a racing driver.

>JAMIE CLARK
>(9 years)

You

You are like the hungry cat
that wants to have fish
He won't wet his claws

> (translated from
> Middle English by
> MICHAEL ROSEN)

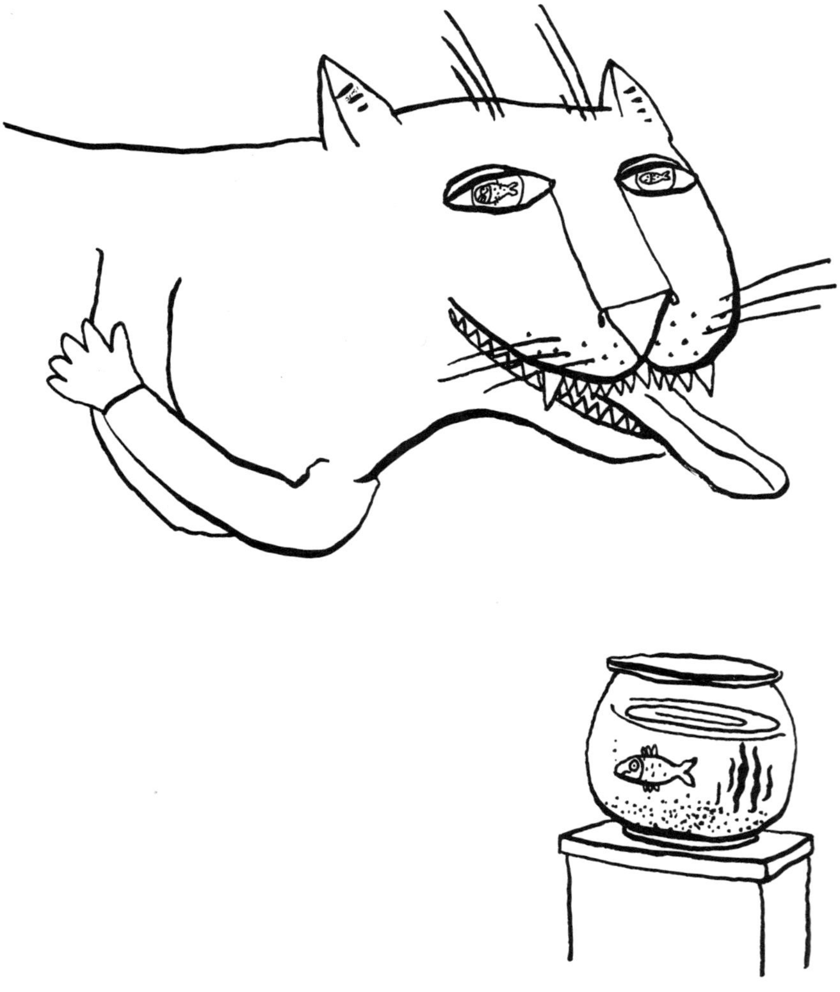

Night Cat

She's there by the fence
but you mustn't call out,
like a scoop of night
or a water shadow
tense for flight
she'll twist and go,
don't open your mouth –
the moon's so close
that the stars blow out –
you turn   she's gone
leaving that patch
where the moon shone
leaving the empty
dress of night
with the stars picked out
and you alone.

                HELEN DUNMORE

Cat

Cat's sneaky,
leaps on my lap
with sudden claws
like nettle stings.

And now she is
tucking herself away –
O so tidily – right down
to her Chinese eyes.

Purrs like a lawn-mower . . .
Yes, but her ears, her ears
are watching something

that hops and twitters
worm-hungry
among the wet petunias.

MATT SIMPSON

Cat and Mouse

Skitterings in the shrubbery,
trembling, twitching leaves.

Cat in shadow. Cat on the lawn.
Still as brick. Intent as the moon.

A pounce, a crash!

Enter Cat with mouse moustache!

MATT SIMPSON

Mouse

Purposeful
cat

purr (puss full)

ALEXIS LYKIARD

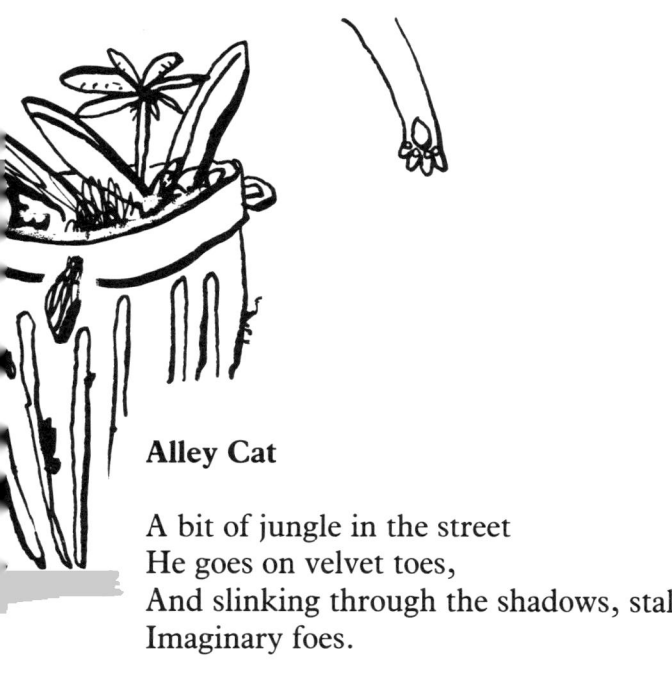

Alley Cat

A bit of jungle in the street
He goes on velvet toes,
And slinking through the shadows, stalks
Imaginary foes.

ESTHER VALCK GEORGES

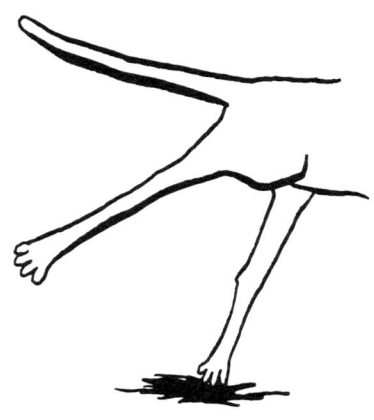

The Cat on the Wall

The cat on the wall
Lies flat on the wall
And her tail lies even flatter.
She has nothing to do
Except look at you
As if nothing you did could matter.

Just once but no more
She may stretch a limp paw
Then slip out her tongue to clean it.
The cat on the wall
Makes you feel rather small
Though she probably doesn't mean it.

JOHN MOLE

Coal Fire in December

It's great
in icy December,
to get home
and chuck off
coat, boots, gloves,
scarf and hat.

And, *ah*,
sit in front of
a glowing coal fire
and hear the warmth
purring like a
contented cat.

WES MAGEE

The Car Park Cat

```
     △                          K
   E   C                      R   C
   H   A                      A   A
   T   R                      P   T
```

Car bonnet cat
keeping warm, car bonnet cat
with crocodile yawn, stares from his sand-
peppered forest of fluff, segment-of-lemon eyes warning,
ENOUGH! Just draw back that hand, retreat, *GO AWAY!*
and his claws flex a tune to say: I won't play but I'll spit
like the sea whipped wild in a gale, hump up like a wave,
flick a forked lightning tail, lash out and scratch at
your lobster-pink face, for no one, *but no one*,
removes from this place, car bonnet cat
keeping warm, car bonnet cat
by the name of
STORM.

GINA DOUTHWAITE

A Warning to Cat Owners

Cats don't have a Highway Code,
They like the freedom of the road.
Our cat, called Zoe, soft and nice,
Ignored the signs and paid the price.
She tried to beat the rush hour traffic,
We fetched a shoe box from the attic.
We dug a grave behind the shed,
And there we laid poor Zoe's head.
We sang a song and gathered flowers,
We cried until the early hours.
But cats don't have a Highway Code,
They like the freedom of the road.

SUE TOWNSEND

A Case of Murder

They should not have left him there alone,
Alone that is except for the cat.
He was only nine, not old enough
To be left alone in a basement flat,
Alone, that is, except for the cat.
A dog would have been a different thing,
A big gruff dog with slashing jaws,
But a cat with round eyes mad as gold,
Plump as a cushion with tucked-in paws –
Better have left him with a fair-sized rat!
But what they did was leave him with a cat.
He hated that cat; he watched it sit,
A buzzing machine of soft black stuff,
He sat and watched and he hated it,
Snug in its fur, hot blood in a muff,
And its mad gold stare and the way it sat
Crooning dark warmth: he loathed all that.
So he took Daddy's stick and he hit the cat.
Then quick as a sudden crack in glass
It hissed, black flash, to a hiding place
In the dust and dark beneath the couch,
And he followed the grin on his new-made face,
A wide-eyed, frightened snarl of a grin,
And he took the stick and he thrust it in,
Hard and quick in the furry dark.
The black fur squealed and he felt his skin
Prickle with sparks of dry delight.
Then the cat again came into sight,
Shot for the door that wasn't quite shut,
But the boy, quick too, slammed fast the door:

The cat, half-through, was cracked like a nut
And the soft black thud was dumped on the floor.
Then the boy was suddenly terrified
And he bit his knuckles and cried and cried;
But he had to do something with the dead thing
   there.
His eyes squeezed beads of salty prayer
But the wound of fear gaped wide and raw;
He dared not touch the thing with his hands
So he fetched a spade and shovelled it
And dumped the load of heavy fur
In the spidery cupboard under the stair
Where it's been for years, and though it died
It's grown in that cupboard and its hot low purr
Grows slowly louder year by year:
There'll not be a corner for the boy to hide
When the cupboard swells and all sides split
And the huge black cat pads out of it.

                                      VERNON SCANNELL

Cat and the Weather

Cat takes a look at the weather:
snow;
puts a paw on the sill;
his perch is piled, is a pillow.

Shape of his pad appears:
will it dig? No,
not like sand,
like his fur almost.

But licked; not liked:
too cold.
Insects are flying, fainting down.
He'll try

to bat one against the pane.
They have no body and no buzz,
and now his feet are wet;
it's a puzzle.

Shakes each leg,
then shakes his skin
to get the white flies off;
looks for his tail,

tells it to come on in
by the radiator.
World's turned queer
somehow: all white,

no smell. Well, here
inside it's still familiar.
He'll go to sleep until
it puts itself right.

    MAY SWENSON

from **A Child's Christmas in Wales**

It was on the afternoon of the day of Christmas Eve, and I was in Mrs Prothero's garden, waiting for cats, with her son Jim. It was snowing. It was always snowing at Christmas. December, in my memory, is white as Lapland, though there were no reindeers. But there were cats. Patient, cold and callous, our hands wrapped in socks, we waited to snowball the cats. Sleek and long as jaguars and horrible-whiskered, spitting and snarling, they would slink and sidle over the white back-garden walls, and the lynx-eyed hunters, Jim and I, fur-capped and moccasined trappers from Hudson Bay, off Mumbles Road, would hurl our deadly snowballs at the green of their eyes.

The wise cats never appeared. We were so still, Eskimo-footed arctic marksmen in the muffling silence of the eternal snows – eternal, ever since Wednesday – that we never heard Mrs Prothero's first cry from her igloo at the bottom of the garden. Or, if we heard it at all, it was, to us, like the far-off challenge of our enemy and prey, the neighbour's polar cat. But soon the voice grew louder. 'Fire!' cried Mrs Prothero, and she beat the dinner-gong.

And we ran down the garden, with the snowballs in our arms, toward the house; and smoke, indeed, was pouring out of the dining-room, and the gong was bombilating, and Mrs Prothero was announcing ruin like a town crier in Pompeii. This was better than all the cats in Wales standing on the wall in a row.

DYLAN THOMAS

Fog

The fog comes
on little cat feet.

It sits looking
over harbor and city
on silent haunches
and then moves on.

CARL SANDBURG

If You,

If you,
Like me,
Were made of fur
And sun warmed you,
Like me,
You'd purr.

KARLA KUSKIN

December Cat

Among the scribbled tangle
of the branches of that garden tree
only about two hundred
lime-coloured leaves still shudder

but the hunting cat
perched in the middle of the scribble
believes he's invisible
to the few sparrows visiting
the tips of the tree

like a giant soldier
standing in a grey street at noon
wearing a bright ginger uniform
hung with guns
hung with grenades
who holds a sprig of heather up
as he shouts to the houses:
Come out! It's all right,
I'm only a hillside!

ADRIAN MITCHELL

Cat

I have walked on the wall
and
have put my eye on the world
and
it had better behave itself.

I have slouched under the bushes
and have made the lumps of feather-covered cat-meat
jump up and down
waving their uneatable bits and squeaking stupidly

I have found slow wriggly things in my earth
and have pulled them with my claws
but they are not much fun
and they are not good cat-meat

I have sat on the flowers, to watch
the big animal that brings me cat-meat
dig holes in my earth
but it was not looking for the wriggly slimy
things that are not cat-meat

It is not as intelligent as a cat,
it does not use its claws to dig
and has nothing to put into the hole
except a stalk of something.

Then it goes. I smell the stalks
and since they are not cat-meat
I stand on them, and dig in my earth
to make it more as I like it

and the big animal is back.
It is jumping up and down
like the feather-covered cat-meat
and waving its uneatable bits
and squeaking stupidly

It is more useless than I'd thought –
for all the jumping and waving it has not managed
to leave the ground and float to the tip of a tree

if it did not bring me cat-meat
I should certainly eat it.

DAVE CALDER

It's Raining Cats and Dogs

Cats are piled in puddles
Dogs are stuck down drains
Cats are in the gutters
And dogs on window panes . . .
   Dogs are on my father
   Cats on Auntie Rose
   A wolfhound on her collar
   And a poodle up her nose . . .
      Pups are on my brother
      A boxer's on his head
      A ginger tom's on Auntie
      A pit bull's stuck on Ted . . .
         There are cats on every car top
         There are dogs on every bike
         There are kittens on my sister
         And pugs all over Mike . . .
            There are labradors in buckets
            There are Pekinese in pails
            Barrels full of barkings
            And rivers wagging tails.

It's really really funny.
It's raining cats and dogs
And tomorrow if we're lucky . . .
It might rain fish and frogs!

                              PETER DIXON

Travel Posters from Thomas Fox Travel Agents

Mice! Feeling trapped? Get away from that dingy old mousehole. Leave your cat behind. Come to the Cheddar Gorge and gorge yourself on its gorgeous local cheeses. Explore its fascinating caverns, homes of the giant mice of long ago. Whisk down to your nearest branch of Thomas Fox Travel Agents and sniff out the facts. Cheese. We aim to please.

Safari Hunting Holidays for cabin-crazy cats. Feline friends. Come to the carefree Cheddar Gorge – mightiest mousetrap in the world. Rodents flock to its cheesy caves. Come hunting to your heart's content. More mice per mile, says your Agent with the smile, Thomas Fox. Slink over for the info.

Dogs! Bored with the bones? Doped out on dog-food? Don't go barking mad. Come to Cheddar for a fun-filled cat-chasing stray-away-day. Cheddar's caverns are crammed with cats. Bound from that basket to book a growlingly good holiday at your local branch of Thomas Fox. Get off that leash. Fetch, boy, fetch!

Tally-Ho Holidays from Thomas Fox.

TONY MITTON

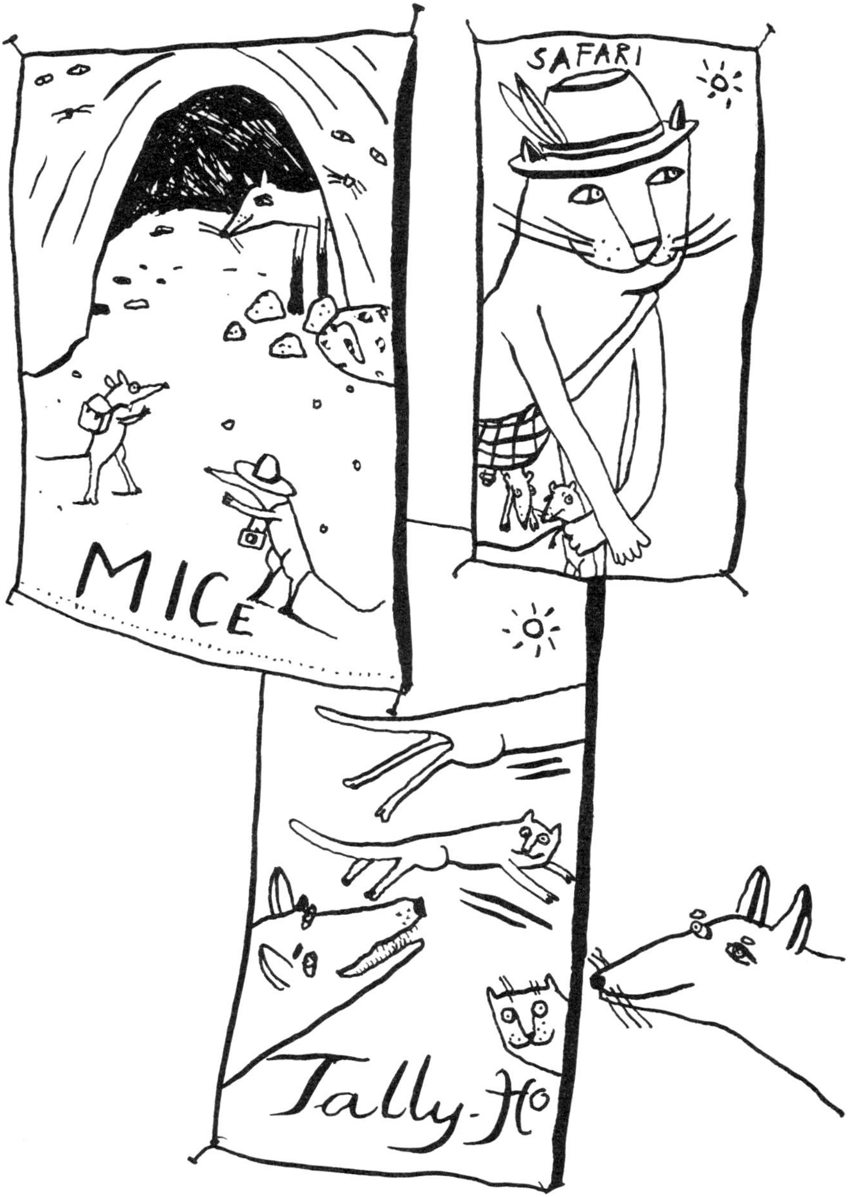
SAFARI
MICE
Tally-Ho

Poem

I can hear the trees whispering
The cat purring
The dogs barking
no wonder I can't get to sleep
I can hear my dad in a rage
tearing up a page
into little bits
while my mother sits
crying
no wonder I can't get to sleep

Susan David
(8 years)

A Little Night Music

I lay awake at midnight
And a smile was on my face
As I heard the caterwauling
Of the cats in Feline Place.
They were bawling, they were yowling,
And they yodelled at the moon.

I grinned a grin: for *my* cat
Was the *only* cat in tune!

I sprang awake at 5 a.m.
The dogs in Canine Square
Were barking out a Bach Chorale
And barking mad they were.
They angered all the neighbourhood
And terrified the birds.

I grinned a grin: for *my* dog,
And *he only*, knew the words!

So

Tickle my funnybone nightly,
Tickle my funnybone, do:
You can't get bamboo shoots at Boots
But you can get Boots shampoo!

Oi!

                                                Kit Wright

Dog's Life

I don't like being me sometimes,
    slumped here
on the carpet, cocking my ears
    every time
someone shuffles or shifts their feet,
    thinking
could be going walkies or getting grub
    or allowed to see
if the cat's left more than a smell
    on her plate.
She's never refused, that cat! Sometimes
    I find myself
dreaming, (twitching my ears, my fur)
    of being just
say *half* as canny as her, with her pert miaow,
    her cheeky tail
flaunting! These people sprawled
    in armchairs
gawping at telly, why don't they play ball
    with me
or enjoy a good nose-licking, eh?

                                               MATT SIMPSON

I Have This Crazy Problem

When I was young
about six years old
I wanted a dog.

I asked my mum and dad
to buy me a dog
but all the time
they would say no.

So from that day onwards
I started to steal dogs.
I would get a dog or two
a day.

Now I am twenty-five years old and
I have collected
about five hundred dogs.

MOHAMMED KHAN

Dogma

Boxers
knock spots off
dalmatians.

Greyhounds
run rings around
lurchers.

Retrievers
are   fetchingly
handsome.

And
    Pointers
           know
                exactly
            where
      they're
going

MARIANNE CHIPPERFIELD

What's the Rush!

'Get up!'
'Get going!'
'Move over!'
'Move off!'

That's my family
bossing each other around in the morning
as the household wakes and shakes itself up.
While Chisel our golden, olden labrador
lies next to a warm, comforting fire
and just – – –
yawns.

'Hurry up!'
'Hurry down!'
'You'll be late!'
'You'll be sorry!'

Shout father, sister, mother and brother
as we zip in and out of
bathroom, bedroom and any room.
While Chisel our golden, olden labrador
brushes the soft, woollen carpet with his tail
and just – – –
closes his eyes.

'How much longer!'
'How much time!'
'Out of my way!'
'Out of the house!'

Doors, cupboards and mouths
fly open and crash shut
until we're all gone.
Except for Chisel our golden, olden labrador
who lazily twitches his rubbery, wet nose
and just – – –
welcomes sleep.

IAN SOUTER

Charlotte's Dog

Daniel the spaniel has ears like rugs,
Teeth like prongs of electric plugs.

His back's a thundery winter sky,
Black clouds, white clouds rumbling by.

His nose is the rubber of an old squash ball
Bounced in the rain. His tail you'd call

A chopped-off rope with a motor inside
That keeps it walloping. Red-rimmed-eyed,

He whimpers like plimsolls on a wooden floor.
When he yawns he closes a crimson door.

When he barks it's a shark of a sound that bites
Through frosty mornings and icy nights.

When he sleeps he wheezes on a dozing lung:
Then he wakes you too with a wash of his tongue!

KIT WRIGHT

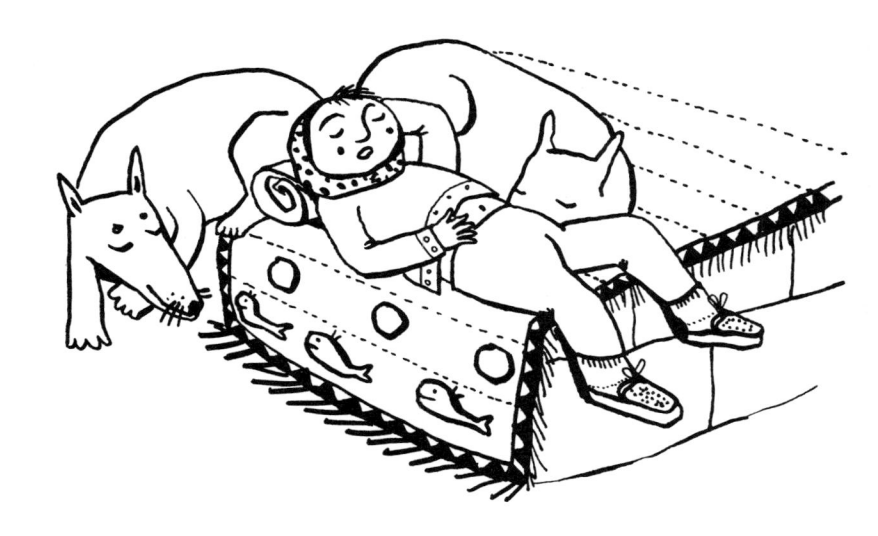

The Mother's Song

It is so still in the house,
There is a calm in the house;
The snowstorm wails out there,
And the dogs are rolled up with snouts under the tail.
My little boy is sleeping on the ledge,
On his back he lies, breathing through his open mouth.
His little stomach is bulging round –
Is it strange if I start to cry with joy?

Eskimo

Solitary Song

Only the air-spirits know
What lies beyond the hills,
Yet I urge my team farther on
Drive on and on,
On and on!

ESKIMO

Haiku

The aged dog
Seems impressed with the song
Of the earth worms.

> Issa
> (translated from
> the Japanese
> by R. H. Blyth)

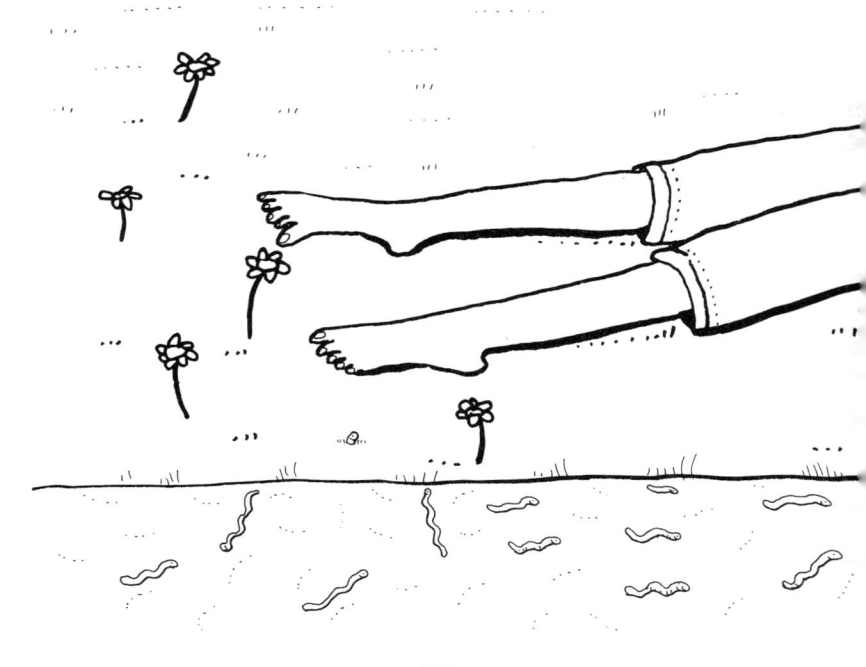

Dog in the Street

dog in the street
stretching
in a nice long yawn –
pure envy
I do likewise

       Ishikawa Takuboku
          (translated from
           the Japanese
         by Carl Sesar)

Doggerel

See me free dog
strutting down the street
nosing in the bins
for a takeaway to eat –
got myself a bad name
messing up the back lane
can't keep my nose clean
sniffing out the rude scene.

House dogs have their leads
yard dogs have their chains.
I'd rather be a free dog
and run hungry in the rain.

See me rough stuff
bag of skin and bone
call no one master
call no where home –
grubby paws, sharp bite,
dodge the law, start fight,
I don't care what man says
this dog will have his day.

House dogs beg and whimper
yard dogs cry all night.
I'd rather be a free dog
and live the way I like.

                    DAVE CALDER

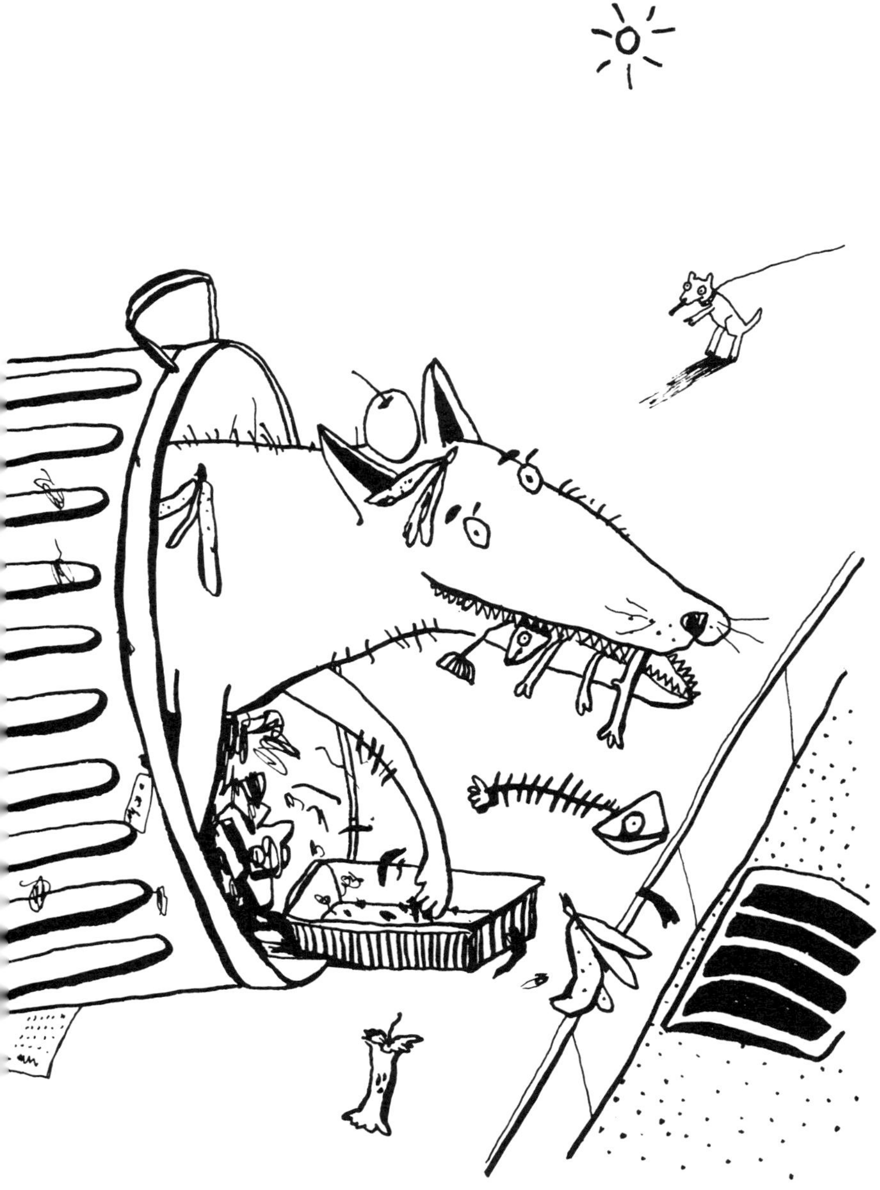

It Takes the (Dog) Biscuit

There's a nasty taste inside my mouth –
My knees have turned to jelly!
I'm right cheesed off, and all because
Our dog has scoffed the telly . . .

I only said the soap star looked
Like mutton dressed as lamb –
But it gave our dog some food for thought
And got me in this jam!

Most dogs put up with bones and scraps,
But not our mongrel, Rover –
He tried to swallow down our set
As I turned the programme over . .

Some politicians, in a stew,
Were being interviewed;
One knew her onions but, alas,
Like all the rest, got chewed!

He takes the cake, our mongrel does –
His taste buds must be bad!
Let's hope his love of TV sets
Is just a currant fad . . .

TREVOR HARVEY

Greedy Dog

This dog will eat anything.

Apple cores and bacon fat,
Milk you poured out for the cat.
He likes the string that ties the roast
And relishes hot buttered toast.
Hide your chocolates! He's a thief,
He'll even eat your handkerchief.
And if you don't like sudden shocks,
Carefully conceal your socks.
Leave some soup without a lid,
And you'll wish you never did.
When you think he must be full,
You find him gobbling bits of wool,
Orange peel or paper bags,
Dusters and old cleaning rags.

This dog will eat anything,
Except for mushrooms and cucumber.

Now what is wrong with those, I wonder?

JAMES HURLEY

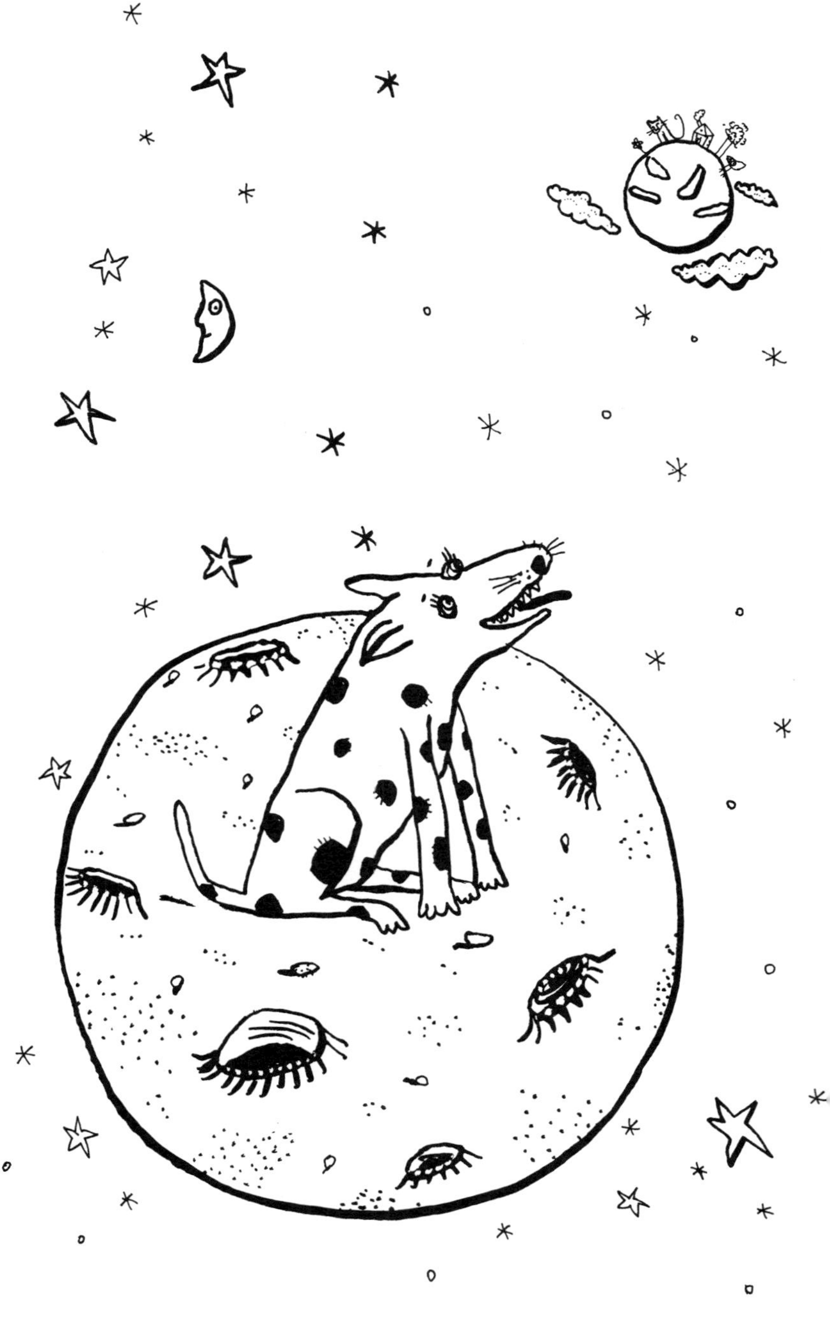

First Dog on the Moon

'Hi there,
First Dog on the Moon.
How do you feel?'

'Like nothing on Earth'

'Yes, but can you taste anything up there?'

*'Bones so cold and dry
They bite my tongue'*

'That's great, First Dog on the Moon.
Now, what can you smell?'

*'Fear of the things hiding
In those hard shadows'*

'OK, OK, So what can you see?'

*'Long dead forests,
broken windows
in empty streets,
Things,
Shadows.'*

'So what are you going to do next,
First Dog on the Moon?'

'Sit and howl at the Earth.'

DAVID ORME

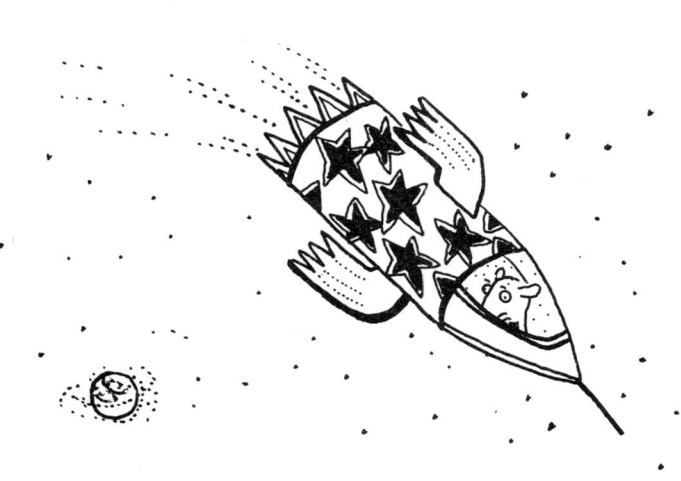

Dog in Space

The barking in space
has died out now,
though dogbones rattle.
And the marks of teeth
on the sputnik's hull
are proof of a battle
impossible to win.
And asteroid-dents
were no help at all.
Did the dog see,
through the window,
earth's blue ball?
Did the dog know
that no other dog
had made that circle
around the earth –
his historic spin
that turned eternal?

MATTHEW SWEENEY

How to Get in the Dog-House

Please follow instructions carelessly:

Take your dog for a walk in the rain.
Borrow as many canine neighbours as possible.
Collect all strays on the way.

Round up regardless of breeding (or lack of it)
and escort down to riverside.

Encourage pack to enjoy itself – i.e.
swim, wallow, roll
and generally envelop its collective body
in the rich alluvial deposits (*mud*)
to be found in tidal estuaries.

Invite back for tea.

Gina Douthwaite

The Barkday Party

For my dog's birthday party
I dressed like a bear.
My friends came as lions
and tigers and wolves and monkeys.
At first, Runabout couldn't believe
the bear was really me. But
he became his old self again
when I fitted on his magician's top hat.
Runabout became the star, running about
jumping up on chairs and tables
barking at every question asked him.
Then, in their ordinary clothes,
my friend Brian and his dad arrived
with their boxer, Skip. And with us
knowing nothing about it, Brian's dad
mixed the dog's party meat and milk
with wine he brought. We started
singing. Runabout started to yelp.
All the other six dogs joined –
yelping
Happy Barkday to you
   Happy Barkday to you
Happy Barkday Runabout
   Happy Barkday to you!

JAMES BERRY

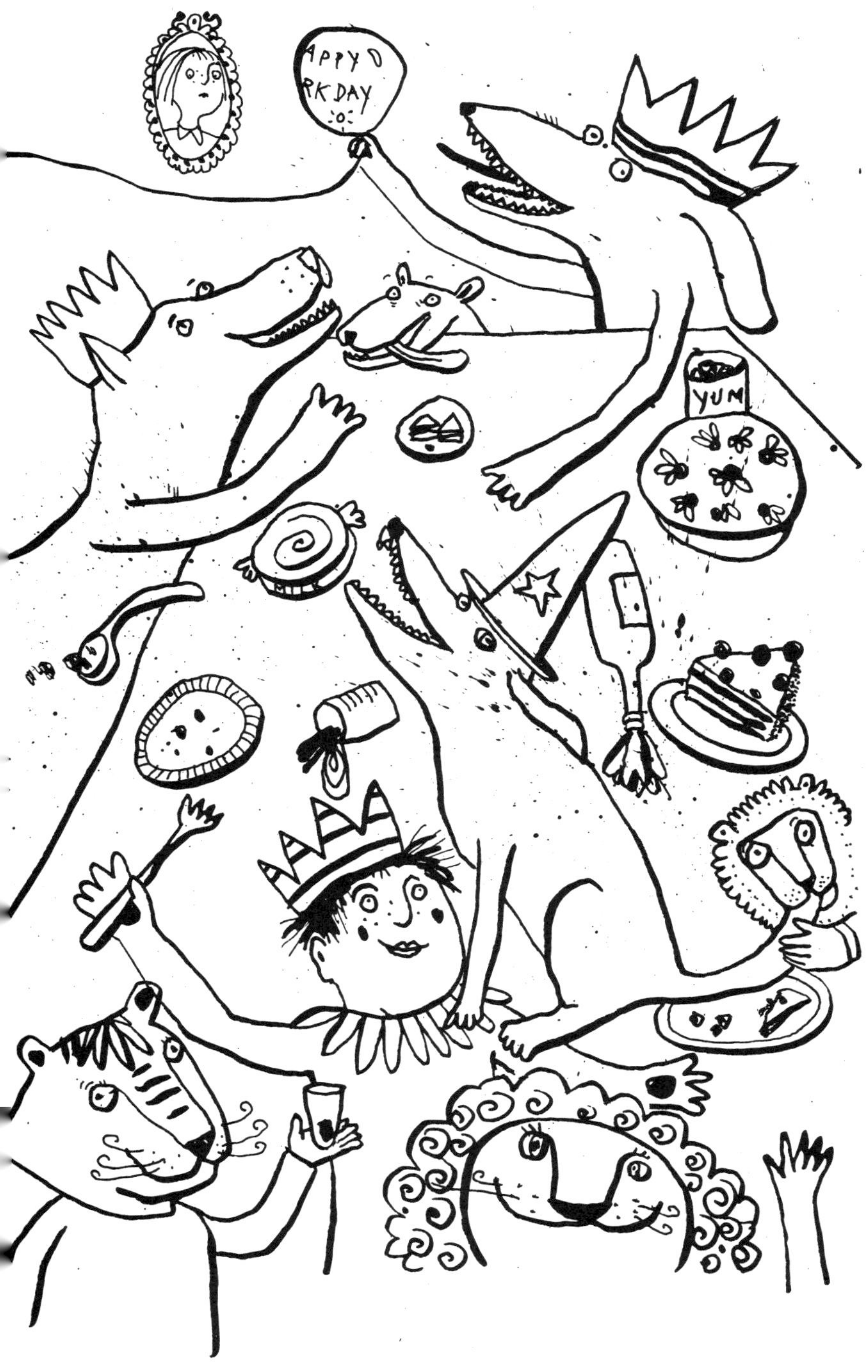
APPY D
RK DAY
YUM

A Dog in the Margin

It seemed like an ordinary sort of poem
As Jim set out
from the top of the page
to visit his Nan.

Nan always bought him
A BIG ICE CREAM
But
The poet had written a surprise for Jim.

Part way down the page a

BIG DOG

bolted from the margin
and tore along the line that Jim had
    reached.

the BIG DOG fastened its teeth around
Jim's terrified arm and
ripped his jumper.

'Help!' screamed Jim.
And there was Nan
dashing across the page
swinging her umbrella.

One whack of that umbrella
and off to safety of the margin raced the

BIG DOG

Resolving to ambush only unarmed
    poems.

Meanwhile,
at the bottom of the page,
Jim ate
A BIG ICE CREAM
through trembling lips,
'It started out like such an ordinary
  poem,'
moaned Jim.
'Don't worry,' said Nan.
'I've repaired your sweater.
No one will ever know.'

JOHN COLDWELL

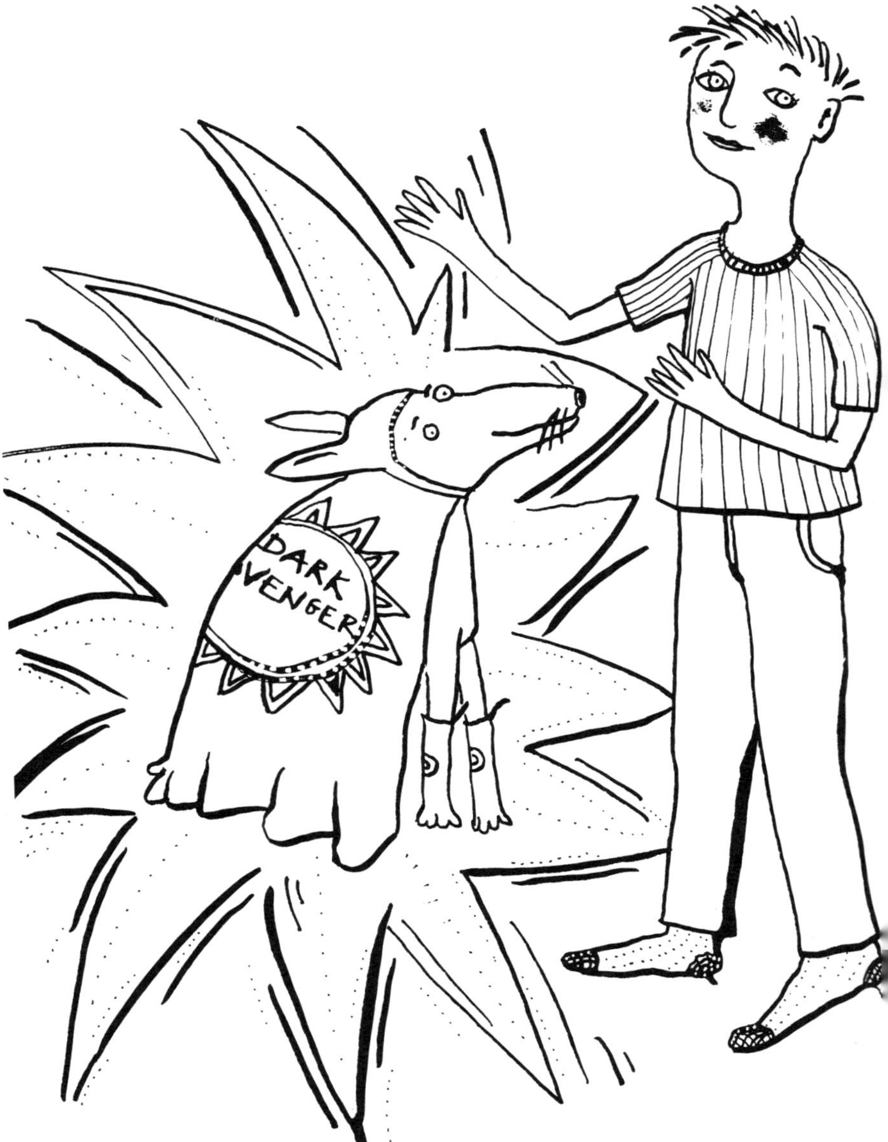
DARK
VENGER

The Dark Avenger

(for 2 voices)

My dog is called The Dark Avenger
Hello, I'm Cuddles

She understands every word I say
Woof?

Last night I took her for a walk
Woof! Walkies! Let's go!

Cleverly, she kept three paces ahead
I dragged him along behind me

She paused at every danger, spying out the land
I stopped at every lamp-post

When the coast was clear, she sped on
I slipped my lead and ran away

Scenting danger, Avenger investigated
I found some fresh chip papers in the bushes

I followed, every sense alert
He blundered through the trees, shouting 'Oy, Come 'ere! Where are you?'

Something – maybe a sixth sense – told me to stop
He tripped over me in the dark

There was a pale menacing figure ahead of us
Then I saw the white Scottie from next door

Avenger sprang into battle, eager to defend his master
Never could stand terriers

They fought like tigers
We scrapped like dogs

Until the enemy was defeated
Till Scottie's owner pulled him off – spoil sport!

Avenger gave a victory salute
I rolled in the puddles

And came to check I was all right
I shook mud over him

'Stop it, you stupid dog!'
He congratulated me

Sometimes, even The Dark Avenger can go too far.
Woof!!

TREVOR MILLUM

I Do Not Understand

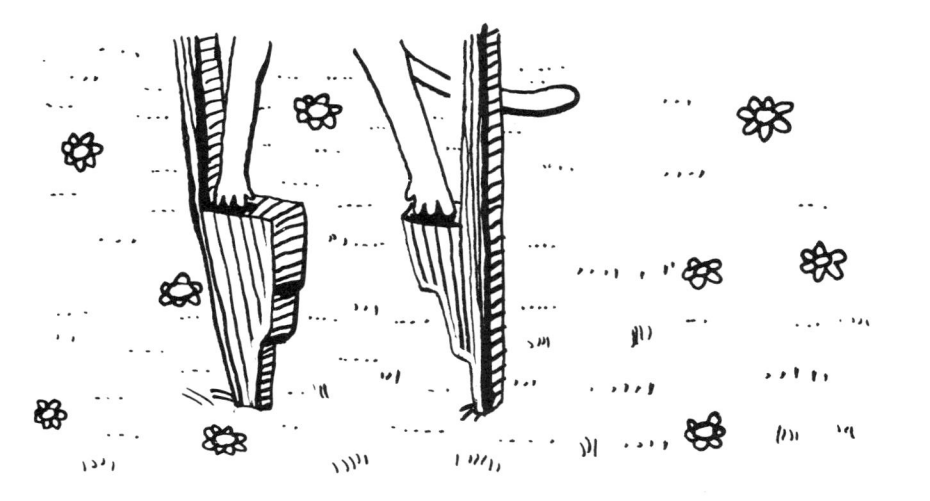

I do not understand
ARF
How people
ARF
GROWL
BARK
Can walk around on two
ARF
Legs.
I see them in the park
BARK
And all around the town.
They walk around on just two legs
Without
BARK
Falling down!
ARF

Karla Kuskin

King of Dogs

I've just been made
King of the Dominion of Dogs.
How frightening.
Why did they pick me,
instead of some Great Dane?
They show me the papers.
It's all above board,
sealed and official.
OK, but I still would like
to finish chewing this stick,
regardless.
Jimbo is explaining
how I need special transport
now that I am a big-shot.
He is hammering away,
installing a royal platform
on the carrier of his bicycle.
You should see the furnishings:
cushions, blankets, carpeting –
la-di-da.

The royal rig-out regalia
has an outfit for all occasions:
knitted caps, football scarves,
colourful vests and assorted straw hats.
Jim attached a plaque
to my royal limo which reads:
King Marv: 1985–?
I sit inside and look
down my snout at everyone.

JULIE O'CALLAGHAN

A Dog's Life

Waking up last Friday and dressing for school
I found I'd turned into a dog.
I looked at myself in the glass.
Same Ben with glasses and broken tooth stared back
But I just knew I was an alsatian.
'You're an alsatian,' I said to my reflection.
'Woof woof,' my reflection barked back.
No doubt about it, I was an alsatian.
I rushed into the bathroom
Where my sister was cleaning her teeth.
'I'm an alsatian,' I barked happily,
'My name's Attila.'
'Stop being stupid,' she said. 'I'm late for school.'
I sank my teeth into this piece of leg
That came out of a nightie.
'Good dog Attila,' she agreed.

I chased downstairs on all fours
Barking joyfully;
Being an alsatian called Atilla agreed with me.
My new life came as a surprise to my mother
Since I have two sisters, a brother and a father
And not one of them is an alsatian.
'Good morning,' I barked to my mother and father
Giving a big grin and letting my tongue loll out.
'I'm an alsatian,' I said,
Standing on my back legs on the chair
And resting my paws in the All Bran.
'Stop dribbling and eat your breakfast properly,'
Said my mother.
'Woof woof,' I explained from my place under the sofa
Trying to eat a sausage without using my front paws.
'Your son's an alsatian,' said my mother.
'Dr McEver said we might see a sudden improvement,'
Said my father from behind his newspaper.
After the first shock, they soon got used to the idea
Of having a dog with spectacles called Attilla
About the house;
Parents can be very adaptable
If you give them a chance.
It's a good life now,
A dog's life.

There's less homework, I don't have to shut doors
And I have my own place on a mat by the fire.
I spend my days sniffing and looking purposeful.
Some days I bury motor bikes
Or bits of sideboard in the cabbage patch.
Baby Sophie likes me a lot;
She gurgles and chuckles as I lick her face
Or try to herd the tortoise into her playpen
Suddenly I feel wanted.
My family speak to me a lot now
And are learning what my barks mean.
'Good boy Attila,' they say and tickle my ears.
My father spends hours taking me for walks
Or throwing sticks for me to bring back in my jaws.
And then to hear my mother calling
On some sunlit afternoon,
'Attila, Attila, time for cubs.'
And I romp up from the garden my tail wagging,
Weaving between the apple trees
And the white sheets on the line.
Well, there's nothing like it.
You really should try it sometime.

GARETH OWEN

Experiment in Puppy Love

I've never snuggled on a lap,
I've never had a cuddle
nor stretched out in the sunshine
nor paddled in a puddle,

I've never sniffed a blade of grass,
I've never gnawed a bone
nor curled up by a fireside
nor chased a stick or stone,

I've never walked upon a lead,
I've never had a name
nor known a home beyond this cage –
just needles, fear and pain.

GINA DOUTHWAITE

The Dog Lovers

So they bought you
And kept you in a
Very good home
Central heating
TV
A deep freeze
A *very* good home –
No one to take you
For that lovely long run –
But otherwise
'A *very* good home.'
They fed you Pal and Chum
But not that lovely long run,
Until, mad with energy and boredom
You escaped – and ran and ran and ran
Under a car.
Today they will cry for you –
Tomorrow they will buy another dog.

Spike Milligan

Burying the Dog in the Garden

When we buried
the dog in
the garden on
the grave we put
a cross and
the tall man
next door was
cross.
'Animals have no
souls,' he said.
'They must have animal
souls,' we said. 'No,'
he said and
shook his head.

'Do you need a
soul to go
to Heaven?' we
asked. He nodded
his head. 'Yes,'
he said.
'That means my
hamster's not
in Heaven,' said
Kevin. 'Nor is
my dog,' I said.
'My cat could sneak
in anywhere,' said
Clare. And we thought
what a strange place Heaven
must be with
nothing to stroke
for eternity.
We were all
seven.
We decided we
did not want to
go to Heaven.
For that the
tall man next
door is to blame.

BRIAN PATTEN

Dead Dog

One day I found a lost dog in the street.
The hairs about its grin were spiked with blood,
And it lay still as stone. It must have been
A little dog, for though I only stood
Nine inches for each one of my four years
I picked it up and took it home. My mother
Squealed, and later father spaded out
A bed and tucked my mongrel down in mud.

I can't remember any feeling but
A moderate pity, cool, not swollen-eyed;
Almost a godlike feeling now it seems.
My lump of dog was ordinary as bread.
I have no recollection of the school
Where I was taught my terror of the dead.

VERNON SCANNELL

April Gale

The wind frightens my dog, but I bathe in it,
Sound, rush, scent of the spring fields.

My dog's hairs are blown like feathers askew,
My coat's a demon, torturing like life.

Ivor Gurney

A Dog in the Quarry

The day was so bright
   that even birdcages flew open.
The breasts of lawns
   heaved with joy
and the cars on the highway
   sang the great song of asphalt.
At Lobzy a dog fell in the quarry
   and howled.
Mothers pushed their prams out of the park opposite
because babies cannot sleep
   when a dog howls,
and a fat old pensioner was cursing the Municipality:
they let the dog fall in the quarry and then leave him there,
and this, if you please, has been going on since morning.

Towards evening even the trees
   stopped blossoming
and the water at the bottom of the quarry
   grew green with death.
But still the dog howled.

Then along came some boys
and made a raft out of two logs
and two planks.
And a man left on the bank
a briefcase . . .
he laid aside his briefcase
and sailed with them.

Their way led across a green puddle
to the island where the dog waited.
It was a voyage like
   the discovery of America,
a voyage like
   the quest of Theseus.
The dog fell silent,
   the boys stood like statues
and one of them punted with a stick,
the waves shimmered nervously,
tadpoles swiftly
   flickered out of the wake,
the heavens
   stood still,
and the man stretched out his hand.

It was a hand
   reaching out across the ages,
it was a hand
   linking
   one world with another,
   life with death,
it was a hand
   joining everything together,
it caught the dog by the scruff of its neck

and then they sailed back
to the music of
an immense fanfare
of the dog's yapping . . .

                    MIROSLAV HOLUB
                      (Czechoslovakian
                      poem translated
                      by GEORGE THEINER)

To My Dog

This gentle beast
This golden beast
laid her long chin
along my wrist

and my wrist
is branded
with her love
and trust

and the salt of my cheek
is hers to lick
so long as I
or she shall last

        ADRIAN MITCHELL

Index of Authors

Simon Armitage   13

James Berry   68
Valerie Bloom   22

Dave Calder   43, 60
Marianne Chipperfield   52
Jamie Clark   23
John Coldwell   70
Sue Cowling   15

Susan David   43
Peter Dixon   45
Gina Douthwaite   32, 67, 81
Helen Dunmore   25

Eskimo   56, 57

Katherine Gallagher   14
Philip Gross   11
Ivor Gurney   86

Trevor Harvey   62
Miroslav Holub   87
James Hurley   63

Issa   58

Mohammed Khan   51
James Kirkup   16
Karla Kuskin   41, 75

Alexis Lykiard   28

Wes Magee   31
Spike Milligan   82
Trevor Millum   73
Adrian Mitchell   42, 90
Tony Mitton   46
John Mole   30
Brian Moses   18

Julie O'Callaghan   76
David Orme   65
Gareth Owen   19, 78

Brian Patten   83

John Rice   20
Michael Rosen   24

Carl Sandburg   40
Vernon Scannell   34, 85
Matt Simpson   26, 27, 50
Ian Souter   53
Matthew Sweeney   66
May Swenson   36

Ishikawa Takuboku   59
Dylan Thomas   38
Sue Townsend   33

Esther Valck Georges   29

Kit Wright   49, 55

Acknowledgements

The author and the publisher would like to thank the following for their kind permission to reprint copyright material in this book:

Simon Armitage for 'Cats' by Simon Armitage, copyright © 1989 Simon Armitage, from *Human Geography* (Smith/Doorstop, 1989); Hamish Hamilton Ltd for 'The Barkday Party' by James Berry, copyright © 1988 James Berry, from *When I Dance* by James Berry (Hamish Hamilton Children's Books, 1988); Valerie Bloom and Cambridge University Press for 'Sun a-Shine, Rain a-Fall' by Valerie Bloom, copyright © 1992 Valerie Bloom, from *Duppy Jamboree and Other Jamaican Poems* (Cambridge University Press, 1992); Dave Calder for 'Cat' by Dave Calder, copyright © 1985 Dave Calder, from *Bamboozled* (Other, 1987) and 'Doggerel' by Dave Calder, copyright © 1993 Dave Calder; Marianne Chipperfield for 'Dogma' by Marianne Chipperfield, copyright © 1994 Marianne Chipperfield; J. E. Clark for 'Cat Drinking' by Jamie Clark, copyright © 1994 Jamie Clark; John Coldwell for 'A Dog in the Margin' by John Coldwell, copyright © 1992 John Coldwell, from *The Bee's Sneeze* (Stride, 1992); Faber and Faber Ltd for 'Litter' by Sue Cowling, copyright © 1991 Sue Cowling, from *What is a Kumquat?* by Sue Cowling (Faber and Faber, 1991); The *Daily Mirror* for 'Poem' by Susan David, copyright © 1970 Susan David, from *The Daily Mirror Children's Literary Competition*; Peter Dixon for 'It's Raining Cats and Dogs' by Peter Dixon, copyright © 1994 Peter Dixon; Gina Douthwaite for 'The Car Park Cat', copyright © 1990 Gina Douthwaite, from *The Usborne Book of Animal Poems* (Usborne, 1990), and for 'Experiment in Puppy Love' and 'How to Get in the Dog-House' by Gina Douthwaite, copyright © 1994 Gina Douthwaite; Helen Dunmore for 'Night Cat' by Helen Dunmore, copyright © 1994 Helen Dunmore, from *Secrets* by Helen Dunmore (Bodley Head, 1994); Katherine Gallagher for her poem 'Feline', copyright © 1994 Katherine Gallagher; Faber and Faber Ltd for 'The Cat's Muse' by Philip Gross, copyright © 1989 Philip Gross, from *Manifold Manor* by Philip Gross (Faber and Faber, 1989); Oxford University Press for 'April Gale' by Ivor Gurney, copyright © 1982 Robin Haines, Sole Trustee of the Gurney Estate, from *Ivor Gurney: Collected Poems* edited by P. J. Kavanagh (OUP, 1982); Trevor Harvey for 'It Takes the (Dog) Biscuit' by Trevor Harvey, copyright © 1992 Trevor Harvey, from *Scrumdiddly* edited by J. Currey (Bodley Head, 1992); Penguin Books Ltd for 'A Dog in the Quarry' by Miroslav Holub, copyright © 1967 Miroslav Holub, translation copyright © 1967 Penguin Books, from *Miroslav Holub: Selected Poems* translated by Ian Milner (Penguin, 1967); James Hurley for 'Greedy Dog' by James Hurley, copyright © 1974 James Hurley, from *If You Should Meet a Crocodile* (Kaye & Ward, 1974); James Kirkup for 'Kitten', an extract from 'Kitten on the Keys' by James Kirkup, copyright © 1994 James Kirkup; HarperCollins Publishers Inc. for 'I Do Not Understand' and 'If You,' by Karla Kuskin, copyright © 1972 Karla Kuskin, from *Any Me I Want To Be* (Harper & Row, 1972); Alexis Lykiard for 'Mouse' by Alexis Lykiard, copyright © 1985, 1994 Alexis Lykiard, from *Cat Kin* (Sinclair-Stevenson, 1994); Wee Magee for 'Coal Fire in December' by Wes Magee, copyright © 1994 Wes Magee; Michael Joseph Ltd for 'The Dog Lovers' by Spike Milligan, copyright © 1972 Spike Milligan Productions Ltd, from *Small Dreams of a Scorpion* by Spike Milligan (Michael Joseph, 1972); Trevor Millum for 'The Dark Avenger' by Trevor Millum, copyright © 1993 Trevor Millum, from *Drama and*

Short Plays (Scholastic, 1993); Peters Fraser & Dunlop for 'December Cat' by Adrian Mitchell, copyright © 1984 Adrian Mitchell, from *On the Beach at Cambridge* by Adrian Mitchell (Allison & Busby, 1984), and for 'To My Dog' by Adrian Mitchell, copyright © Adrian Mitchell, from *All My Own Stuff* by Adrian Mitchell (Simon & Schuster). None of Adrian Mitchell's poems are to be used in connection with any exam whatsoever; Tony Mitton for 'Travel Posters from Thomas Fox Travel Agents' by Tony Mitton, copyright © 1994 Tony Mitton; Penguin Books Ltd for 'The Cat on the Wall' by John Mole, copyright © 1990 John Mole, from *Catching the Spider* by John Mole (Blackie Children's Books, 1990); Brian Moses for 'Next Door's Cat' by Brian Moses, copyright © 1994 Brian Moses; Julie O'Callaghan for 'King of Dogs' by Julie O'Callaghan, copyright © 1994 Julie O'Callaghan; David Orme for 'First Dog on the Moon' by David Orme, copyright © 1994 David Orme; HarperCollins Publishers Ltd for 'A Dog's Life' by Gareth Owen, copyright © 1985 Gareth Owen, from *Song of the City* by Gareth Owen (HarperCollins Young Lions, 1985), and for 'The Owl and the Astronaut' by Gareth Owen, copyright © 1986 Gareth Owen, from *The Kingfisher Book of Comic Verse*, ed. Roger McGough (HarperCollins, 1986); Penguin Books Ltd for 'Burying the Dog in the Garden' by Brian Patten, copyright © 1985 Brian Patten, from *Gargling With Jelly* by Brian Patten (Viking Kestrel, 1985); John Rice for 'The Cat Sat on the Mat' by John Rice, copyright © 1990 John Rice; Penguin Books Ltd for 'You' translated by Michael Rosen, translation © 1979 Michael Rosen; Harcourt Brace and Company Inc. for 'Fog' by Carl Sandburg, copyright © 1944 Carl Sandburg, from *Chicago Poems* by Carl Sandburg (Harcourt Brace, 1944); Robson Books Ltd for 'A Case of Murder' and 'Dead Dog' by Vernon Scannell, copyright © 1965 Vernon Scannell, both from *New and Collected Poems 1950–1980* by Vernon Scannell (Robson Books, 1980); Matt Simpson for 'Cat', 'Cat and Mouse' and 'Dog's Life' by Matt Simpson, copyright © 1993 Matt Simpson, all from *The Pigs' Thermal Underwear* by Matt Simpson (Headland, 1993); Ian Souter for 'What's the Rush!' by Ian Souter, copyright © 1994 Ian Souter; Matthew Sweeney for 'Dog in Space' by Matthew Sweeney, copyright © 1994 Matthew Sweeney; HarperCollins Publishers Ltd for 'Cat and the Weather' by May Swenson, copyright © 1989 May Swenson, from *The Song That Sings the Bird* edited by Ruth Craft (HarperCollins, 1989); Kodansha International Ltd for 'Dog in the Street' by Ishikawa Takuboku, translated by Carl Sesar, copyright © 1966 Kodansha International Ltd, from *Poems to Eat* by Ishikawa Takuboku, translated by Carl Sesar (Kodansha, 1966); David Higham Associates Ltd for the extract from *A Child's Christmas in Wales* by Dylan Thomas (J. M. Dent, 1954), copyright © 1954 the Trustees for the copyrights of the late Dylan Thomas; Sheil Land Associates for 'A Warning to Cat Owners' by Sue Townsend, copyright © 1991 Sue Townsend, from *Casting a Spell*, ed. Angela Huth (Orchard, 1991); Kit Wright for 'A Little Night Music' by Kit Wright, copyright © 1994 Kit Wright; Penguin Books Ltd for 'Charlotte's Dog' by Kit Wright, copyright © 1984, 1987 Kit Wright, from *Cat Among the Pigeons* (Viking Kestrel, 1987).

Every effort has been made to trace the copyright holders, but the author and publisher apologize if any inadvertent omission has been made.